ANIMAL LIFE IN THE DESERT

DESERT ANIMALS

Lynn M. Stone

Rourke Publications, Inc.
Vero Beach, Florida 32964

Edited by Pamela J.P. Schroeder

PHOTO CREDITS
Photo p. 13 © Joe McDonald; all other photos © Lynn M. Stone

ACKNOWLEDGEMENT
The author thanks the staff of the Arizona-Sonora Desert Museum,
Tucson, for its cooperation with some of the photography in
this book.

Library of Congress Cataloging-in-Publication Data
Stone, Lynn M.
  Animal life in the desert / by Lynn Stone.
      p.   cm. — (Desert animals)
  Summary: Describes the lives and interaction of animals and
plants in the desert.
  ISBN 0-86625-631-8
  1. Desert animals—Juvenile literature. 2. Desert ecology—
Juvenile literature. [1. Desert ecology. 2. Ecology.]
I. Title. II. Series: Stone, Lynn M.   Desert animals.
QL116.S76   1997
591.754—dc21   97-16382
                                             CIP
                                             AC

Printed in the USA

TABLE OF CONTENTS

DESERTS

The deserts of America's West and Southwest are hot and dry for much of the year. They have no more than 12 inches (31 centimeters) of rain or snow. Deserts can go a long time without any rain or snow.

Some deserts are warmer than others. How warm a desert is and when it has rainfall have much to do with what plants grow there. Desert plants, in turn, have much to do with which animals live in the deserts.

Fog bathes the greening Sonoran Desert on a morning in early spring.

ANIMALS IN THE DESERTS

No desert is as lifeless as it may seem on a hot, summer day. Even in this dry world, many animals make a living.

Plants, in one way or another, are food for animals. The deserts with the most plants have the greatest variety and numbers of animals.

Much of North America's West is desert. The Sonoran Desert in Arizona has two periods of yearly rain, and it lies in a warm climate. The warmth and timing of the rain help plants grow. It is the region with the most plants and animals.

A colorful collared lizard male crawls from its winter den. Warmer weather and longer days awake hibernating desert animals, like the lizard.

FOOD-MAKERS

When desert plants and animals die, other animals and even tiny **bacteria** (bak TEER ee ah) eat them. The dead animals and plants **decay** (deh KAY). Their **nutrients** (NU tree ents) go back into air, water, and soil.

Nutrients are things that living **organisms** (OR ga ni zemz)—plants and animals—need to grow and live. Plants grow by using nutrients from air, water, soil, and even sunlight.

As in forests, prairies, and even the ocean, plants are food-makers for animals in the desert.

Desert plants, like these prickly pear cactus, provide food for animals, like the peccary, or javelina.

PLANT-EATERS

Some desert animals grow by eating plants. A beetle, for example, may nibble on cactus. A desert bighorn sheep may eat grass.

These animals and many more are **herbivores** (ERB uh vorz), or plant-eaters. The largest herbivores are the bighorn and the piglike peccary, or javelina (hah vel EE nuh).

They grow and get energy from eating berries, leaves, fruits, stems, and other plant parts.

A desert bighorn, one of the largest desert herbivores, chews on its cud.

The American deserts have a great variety of animals, like this "furry" tarantula, a cousin of spiders and scorpions.

The Mexican beaded lizard, here with an egg it has eaten, is a desert predator. It's one of two poisonous lizards in the world.

HUNTERS AND HUNTED

Predators (PRED uh torz), the animal hunters, live by attacking and eating other animals. They may eat plant-eating animals or smaller predators. In one way or another, even predators depend on sunlight and plants for their food.

A desert snake, for example, may eat a plant-eating mouse. Some of the plant's food energy moves through the mouse to the snake. When a coyote catches the snake, the plant's food energy moves again to the coyote.

The desert screech owl is a predator who preys on plant-eating rodents.

THE WARM MONTHS

Most desert animals cannot live in extremely warm or cold weather. As seasons change, animals change how they live.

On the Sonoran Desert in Arizona, spring begins in late February. Daylight time grows longer. The air warms and winds increase. The desert blooms. Many insects hatch and grow. Animals have fresh, new sources of food.

Hot days begin in May. Daytime temperatures climb above 105° F (41° C). Animals stay in shade or retreat to burrows. Many go out only at night.

Thunderstorms rock the Sonoran in summer. The desert then gets a small drink and cools a little at night.

16

The Inca dove and other birds begin to look for nesting places when spring weather warms the desert.

THE COOL MONTHS

Desert nights, even in summer, can be quite cool. By October, days are cool, too.

Snow brushes northern deserts in North America. Many animals **hibernate** (HI ber nayt) to escape the cold. Ground squirrels, lizards, snakes, and tortoises crawl into burrows to sleep winter away.

In winter, the Sonoran gathers moisture again— from gentle rains rather than storms. Snow is rare on the Sonoran, but nights are chilly. Sometimes the temperature dips below freezing.

Cool autumn days drive snakes, like this sidewinder, and lizards into hibernation. Most rodents also hibernate.

WHERE TO SEE DESERT ANIMALS

Several Western and Southwestern states have desert country. Some of the best places to see Sonoran Desert animals are in Arizona's Saguaro National Park and Organ Pipe National Monument. The Arizona-Sonora Desert Museum, a wonderful zoo and garden, is in Tucson, Arizona.

California has Death Valley and Joshua Tree National Parks and the huge Anza-Borrego Desert State Park. These parks are largely within the Mojave Desert.

Big Bend National Park in Texas is a good place to see Chihuahuan Desert animals.

Organ Pipe National Monument in Arizona is a great place to see wild plants and animals of the Sonoran Desert.

DESERT ANIMALS AND PEOPLE

Deserts in America are changing. As desert cities like Las Vegas, Tucson, and Phoenix grow, the desert around them shrinks. People scrape deserts clear for new homes and fields of fruits and vegetables. They bring water to the fields with pipes and canals.

Tracks from off-road vehicles, military exercises, and too much grazing by livestock also hurt the desert.

It's good that desert parks protect much of the desert and its animal life.

Glossary

bacteria (bak TEER ee ah) — a group of tiny living things that can be seen only with a microscope, both helpful and harmful to people

decay (deh KAY) — rotting away, breaking down

herbivore (ERB uh vor) — a plant-eating animal

hibernate (HI ber nayt) — to enter the deep, sleeplike condition in which some animals spend the winter

nutrient (NU tree ent) — any of several "good" substances that the body needs for health, growth, and energy; vitamins and minerals

organism (OR ga nih zem) — any living thing

predator (PRED uh tor) — an animal that kills other animals for food

INDEX